Dearest
Jackie,

Blossom
Into Your Unique Self

The Power of Creating
Holistic Wealth

Falguni Katira

Thank you for helping me
Blossom into my unique
Self. Here's wishing you a lot
of blossoming in all areas of
your life. keep inspiring.
Big Love,
Falguni

Book Cover & Logo Design: Falguni Katira

Book Coach: Linda Vettrus-Nichols
www.LindaVettrus-Nichols.com

DEDICATION

I dedicate this book to every human being who has
not given up on life.

All of you who continue to repair yourselves through
all the challenges and obstacles you've faced.

Keep pairing back to the source.

TABLE OF CONTENTS

ACKNOWLEDGMENTS

PRAISE

INTRODUCTION

BLOSSOM

NOTE FROM THE AUTHOR

RESOURCE ARTICLES

ABOUT THE AUTHOR

ACKNOWLEDGMENTS

As I share my life experiences in this book, it is important for me to acknowledge the many people who helped me become the person I am today. Like the list of invitees to a wedding, short listing becomes difficult.

My deepest gratitude to my spiritual master, Pujya Rameshbhai Oza (Bhaishri), for being the torchbearer of wisdom and love in my life.

To my dearest sons Vivaan & Aaditya that changed my life altogether and gave it a deeper meaning.

To my beloved husband Gopal Bhagia who's been a pillar of support and a catalyst for turning this caterpillar into a butterfly.

To my sources of inspiration, my super supportive and always encouraging parents and in-laws who have had an unflinching belief in me.

To my two sisters Geeta and Ami for being my support system. Thank you for guiding me and being my sounding board during this book writing process.

To my extended family, friends, and Musketeers who have always encouraged me to give my best.

To my encouraging and supportive followers, thank you for believing in me.

PRAISE FOR
BLOSSOM INTO YOUR
UNIQUE SELF

"Falguni Katira has created a powerful guide to help you Blossom to your full potential. Her relatable style and courageous personal story, combined with strategic, practical exercises, will help you drop your excuses and create your abundant life."

~Kristin. A. Sherry
International Best Selling Author & Creator of YouMap®

"Imagine you are on the ground floor of a tall office building looking out a westward facing window. You continue upward to the tenth, twentieth, and fortieth floors and look westward. With each successive height you reach, though you're looking in the same direction, what you can see has changed dramatically. That's what reading Falguni's book is like. It will raise your level of awareness as you read and absorb its lessons. And you'll never go back to the bottom floor again."

~Bob Sager
Founder, SpearPoint Solutions

"Every step in this book has purpose and a subtle transformation. Falguni is my go-to person when I want to learn about spiritual practices that I can apply in my busy schedule. Her knowledge, wisdom and skill in the area of holistic abundance is deep and wide. She is one in a million."

~Mary Henderson
Personal Brand & Digital Business Specialist

INTRODUCTION

"Why me?" That's the question nobody could answer.

How many times have you heard that question from yourself or others?

When I started my journey within, I realized that I had so many strengths. Before that I was always thinking, 'Oh, I'm not so smart and what do I have to give?' I eventually lost my sense of value and worth. When everything in my life started to fall apart, I asked myself, 'Am I a nobody now? Does anybody even see me?'

So, to gain my visibility back, I slowed down to really see myself. I started to spend long moments in front of the mirror just looking at me and taking in every fine detail. Then I started talking to myself, the one in the mirror, and saying kind things. I started to fall in love with my own self for the very first time.

Imagine living in this particular body for so many years and not really knowing her.

So that's where it started for me. As I stepped into my unique nature I was like, 'Okay, you can't take this person lightly at all. She's the real deal.' As I learned to love myself more and more, I couldn't help but share 'me' authentically with others. When you have enough and when you know enough, you can't help but share.

Knowing my true self was extremely important for me.

Knowing true self is about knowing who you are at a spiritual level and at the very practical level. This helped me to understand my limitations.

Understanding my weaknesses and my strengths was extremely eye opening and critical for my growth. Are you feeling good about who you are? Are you feeling good about where you are in life? If so... is this feeling increasing each day? When we start appreciating the good things that are happening, we finally start seeing them as a blessing that we deserve.

The more I understand the experiences of my life, the more I understand that we are all influencers at every level. Our kids, partners, parents, extended family, and friends are impacted by us no matter what. Therefore, we can never say enough, do enough or give back enough to this world. It is a world that constantly keeps us on our toes and keeps giving us the gift of experience.

I am now a Personal Growth Strategist and Certified Transformation Coach who empowers leaders on their path towards holistic growth and success. My *Journey to Visibility* podcast brings inspiration from the VICTORY stories and personal experiences of various leaders.

I now understand that my life's purpose is to create a ripple effect of radical self-awareness, bringing true joy and passion into the lives of others. I believe that all individuals are the torchbearers of culture and stewardship.

Leaders who work with me are positioned to maintain their competitive edge in the face of global change.

Despite hundreds of posts, thousands of reactions, and millions of views on social media... I still felt there was so much more I had to share. That's when I realized I had not shared my personal story of transformation. This is what brought about the idea of writing this book. I trust you will enjoy my story.

"The life we live is the example we give."

~ Falguni Katira

CHAPTER 1

Keep Growing & Giving

I lived a wonderful life in India. From the outside in it was a life many aspired to live. But, for me, it was a rather sheltered life because I was living with my parents. We were a close-knit family. My parents created a very protective, nice environment for my two younger sisters and me. They created a little ecosystem containing our extended family members, their friends, and the children of their friends.

The sheltered life that my parents had built for me was with all the right intentions and for all the right reasons. They wanted to protect their girls, probably more than if we had been boys. I feel like my parents did everything with the most positive intent.

The first shock that I experienced in life was attending college at age fifteen and finding this world to be dramatically different from my own. When I started to meet other people outside of my parent's eco circle, the reality of what was really going on in the world took hold. I felt like a little bit of an outcast and I was extremely judgmental of anyone who was not from my ecosystem.

There were many more shocks to follow.

When I found the freedom of being able to separate and differentiate from others, I started to actually get in touch with myself. I started asking the question, "Do I want to do this?"

My friends would decide to go see a movie and they would invite me to go along. I gave myself the freedom to ask, "Do I want to go with my friends to this particular movie?" If they were eating and offered me a bite, I now had the freedom to ask myself, "Do I want to eat this food?" or even "Do I want to eat right now?"

The first time I checked in with myself, it felt a little scary and at the same time very powerful. I also realized that up until that point I was living a rather mindless life.

Let's do this, let's do that... and it was all my parent's ideas. My parents took really good care of their children in terms of giving us a social life. They of course controlled that social life. We each had our friends within that eco-chamber. So, things got rather interesting when I got out of all of that and started to make friends of my own. I was so situated into my own self and in the way I had been brought up that everything we didn't do, in my mind, was wrong. That's what I was believing.

One of my sisters was studying and living far from home. My dad and I were visiting her. She was living in a college dorm and I had never lived like that. I had always lived at home with my parents and studied in the same city. I never did end up living the dorm life.

In experiencing this way of living, my sister got to meet people from all over India, which is a place where people speak seventeen different languages and nine hundred different dialects.

All of my sister's friends came from different cultures, religions, and ways of being. Indian culture is one of the oldest, richest cultures known to man.

India is the land of mystery and diversity. It has the height of the Himalayas and the depth of the Indian Ocean. India also contains an astonishing variety of geographical features: eternally frozen glaciers, deep rainforests, fertile valleys, blistering deserts, and even palm sprinkled silvery beaches.

Ideologies are also different there with so many gods that are worshipped depending on your religion. It's a wonderful amalgamation of all these ideologies... all these different preferences and choices. This is what makes living in India unique.

When my father and I went to visit my sister, my father took us out to dinner and included my sister's friends. Everyone was of course free to order whatever they wanted.

One of the girls ordered fish, which is considered meat in my family's way of thinking. It also has its own smell. My father and I looked at each other as we smelled that fish, and because of our own limitations we could not take a bite of our food. Then we looked at my sister sitting next to her friend acting as if everything was normal. She wasn't pretending things were okay, this was the norm in her new movie. In her new reality. My sister just sat there eating the food she had ordered, which was vegetarian.

This was the first time I realized that my sister had grown up. I was the older one, and yet she was the one who had actually grown up. I felt extremely uncomfortable as we were walking back to our hotel. I said, "Dad, she's grown up!" My dad stopped and turned towards me. He looked me in the eye and said, "I agree". "I really think she's getting adjusted to things."

As a parent he was also getting adjusted to things. I'm sure it wasn't the first time for him like it was for me.

That was a very pivotal moment in my life.

CHAPTER 2

Learn More About Your True Self

I finally realized that I could completely accept people in my world who were different, and I started accepting them more and more. I stopped resisting and started to understand that when I had true feelings for somebody, I could overlook our differences.

I never knew lack. The world to me was about abundance and I never had to worry about anything.

I was the first woman to get her master's degree in my extended family. It wasn't really regarded very highly because we're from a business community. My dad is also not that highly educated. He is a very successful businessman with a very strong business acumen. He knows the ins and outs of stuff. I was given an option after I graduated from school to go to college or get married. I am thankful that I chose to go to college.

r college, I had a wonderful career. My dad had expected that out of all my siblings, I would want to join his business. I was the one who wanted to do something different and chose a different career path.

I wanted to get into the marketing and advertising world. After college, I was able to get a paid internship at an advertising agency. It was a great opportunity that really launched my career. I remember getting that first paycheck as an intern, it wasn't much but I was thrilled. I remember walking in the door and showing it to my parents. It was like I had won a big medal or something. They said, "That's wonderful. Do whatever you want with it."

For some reason I started thinking that they were not happy for me and they didn't want me to grow. Again, that was very naive of me when I think about it now. At that point, that was my belief. I continued forming those kinds of beliefs. I didn't consider the context or thought process behind my parent's comments or actions.

So that's how my life was in India until I decided to get married.

Then when I experienced true feelings for my husband... boyfriend at that point... I was like, 'okay, he lives far away from me now. A man from India who was living in America. He's always been traveling, eats meat, and drinks alcohol'. He was totally different from any man I had ever known.

The entire maternal and paternal side of my family lived within walking distance. So, to be able to move to a completely foreign country only knowing this one man was huge for me and my family.

That's a story in itself of how my parents dealt with me choosing this man and agreeing to that marriage, especially since we were not from the same cultural background. He's an Indian and yet our cultures were very different. So, to get married to him and go to America was a real feat.

In the first place, it took some daring to go.

I wanted to get married to him so bad. Still living a bit in that not very mindful life, I had never bothered to ask my boyfriend exactly where he lived or where he was employed and how much he made. This is quite embarrassing to admit, seeing that we dated for ten years in secret.

Telling my parents that I wanted to get married to somebody who lived in America, a place none of our family members had ever visited, was crazy to them. In India we of course would hear things about America. We also watched American movies... it was such a progressive world there. You never know if you can trust people outside your circle let alone living outside of your country.

When I told my dad that I completely trusted this man,

he asked me three fundamental questions: Where does he work? How much does he earn? And where does he live?

Fair enough. This was the minimum he needed to know about whom I wanted to marry. The problem was that I had never thought to ask my boyfriend about those details, even though I talked to him every day. This is how delusional I was that all these things didn't matter.

Nothing was greater than love in my mind.

I answered my dad's questions with whatever I remembered hearing. My boyfriend was living in Delaware. I couldn't quite remember that word, so I said Denver because that's where a Bollywood actress I knew about was living. For the company name I gave him some random name, which of course did not exist. I translated the American dollar ratio to Indian rupees and made up a figure as to how much my boyfriend made in a year.

That was all such a disaster, you can imagine my plight.

I went to work that day and when I got home that evening my father confronted me. He said, "You know nothing! Do you even know his name? You gave me all wrong answers. These are the right answers" And I was really taken aback.

Long story short, I didn't budge.

We both wanted to get married so bad that all of the embarrassment became part of my victory story.

When I finally revealed who this man was, I said, "You remember him. Right? He went to my high school and was my senior. You've even met his family. My father thought for a moment and said, "Oh, yes I do vaguely remember that young man."

What my dad didn't know is that my boyfriend, soon to be my husband, had returned to India every other year to see me. We didn't start dating until after he had graduated from college and had gotten a job in Africa, then eventually moved to America.

When he arrived in India, November 18th, we went straight to the courthouse and got married in order to start the processing for my visa.

He was a bit nervous to meet my parents. Everyone got along quite well, and we had a beautiful engagement ceremony November 25th and wedding November 28th with his family and mine. My visa arrived December 6th.

We flew to America and landed at an airport in New York City. It was Christmas Day and so it was a wonderful time of the year to be in the US.

My life changed completely that day, but the reality had not sunk in yet.

I enjoyed the honeymoon phase of life.

Eventually I realized that I had not only halted my thriving career I would be starting over.

I had been so excited to get married and become his wife that I forgot about being a career-oriented woman. I arrived in America on a dependent visa, only because it was the quickest way. That meant I was not able to work or attend college without paying a higher tuition.

Reality did not sink in until January when my husband was at work all day and I had nothing to do.

How much time did I need to chat with my parents or friends back home anyways?

CHAPTER 3
You Have Full Potential

Not knowing our neighbors was also a challenge for me. The daily habits of my life had been severely interrupted, and this was also interfering with my married life. As a new wife I was dealing with interpersonal rifts with my husband. Since I wasn't working, I was not able to empathize with him coming home from work being tired. I wanted him to pay attention to me and talk with me. In hindsight it all makes sense, however at that point it was not making sense at all. So, it was a really challenging time for both of us.

I didn't want to fight I wanted a change. I started volunteering and meeting people. I desperately wanted to blend-in, and I wanted to learn so much about my new world. I was hyper aware in-regards to the way I looked and sounded. Speaking with a heavy accent brought on a bit of anxiety and feelings of insecurity.

As I continued meeting people, I thought my new American acquaintances had something that I didn't. I forgot to see the fact that others were learning something from me as well. I brought something different to the table. At that point in time, I didn't understand that when you operate in fear, you lose.

I started to lose my senses to understand and think logically. I started doing odd jobs, which I had never imagined I'd do. Once I was able to change my citizen status, I ended up studying, and that's how I got my master's degree in communication and business management with a 4.0 GPA. When I stepped into the corporate world, I felt like I was truly living again. As I started to rise up the corporate ladder, the rifts with my husband dramatically reduced.

I now have a good career in the US and all of that turned out to be absolutely fine.

Family Life

My career was really doing great. I had a fabulous job, everything was working. Getting and staying pregnant was another story. I was not able to get pregnant, so we went to multiple doctors to see what was going on, nothing was wrong and yet nothing happened. One fine day out of nowhere, I became pregnant.

I went into labor when I was six months pregnant.

My little girl did not survive.

I got pregnant for a second time and lost that baby too. This was a very painful tubal pregnancy, which almost took my life.

I got pregnant again and lost that baby in the first twelve weeks.

By the fourth pregnancy, the challenge was to stay pregnant.

Working pregnant and going to doctor appointments once a week was exhausting. That only lasted for six months when the doctor told me to park myself in a hospital bed for the last three months of that high-risk pregnancy. I was instructed to keep my feet off the ground until I delivered the baby. I was only twenty-four weeks into my pregnancy at that time. It was a tumultuous journey that ended in a miracle birth.

We had a beautiful baby boy!

Despite another high-risk pregnancy, I was able to have a second child as well. So basically, it took five pregnancies to produce two kids, our two boys.

After getting through a full-term pregnancy and delivering our second child, I was overcome with the bliss of motherhood once again. My parents came for a visit and it was so much fun to introduce them to their new grandson.

Six days later I realized that my husband had been seeing someone else. I was postpartum and super hormonal, so things got really uncomfortable from there. I pretended that everything was alright and that I had it all together.

Little by little the whole thing sank in and I figured out what had been going on. The emotions of being in that place of knowing about my husband's infidelity with a woman, where we both worked and who lived close to us was insane.

As the weeks went on, I felt so full of emotions with nowhere to turn. At that time, I had chosen not to talk to anyone about the situation with my husband. There were a million dialogues playing out in my head. I decided to journal about what had happened and how I felt about the whole crazy mess.

I finally confronted my husband. He was initially in complete denial. After a series of intense conversations and night long discussions, I gathered my courage and told him that he was free to leave the marriage. This was another very pivotal moment in my life. It actually changed the trajectory of my life. It was the first time I was really thinking about me. I had always lived in someone else's eco-chamber. If I really think about it... that's the way I was raised.

My parents returned to India, completely unaware of what had transpired.

CHAPTER 4
When You Grow, You Give

When I started to do regular check ins with myself, I got deeper into meditation. I was already very spiritually inclined. My life circumstances elevated my sense of spirituality. I started to enjoy spiritual practices that brought me all of the strength that I needed to skim through these situations.

When I look back, I can see that I was actually being held. It reminds me of the story where you see two sets of footprints in the sand and then you only see one. That's like my story. When you don't understand your circumstances, God is actually carrying you at that point. So even when you have given up on yourself... God has not.

When I started to feel richer within, I started to realize that it was extremely unfair to keep all that wealth to myself. So, I started to give.

When you have something extremely valuable, you start to give it to people around you.

You're my friend, I want to share this with you.

So, all of the churning that was happening within me, I started sharing that sweet little butter with those around me.

Then once they started to benefit, I started giving even more. I noticed that the more I gave, the more I received. I come to giving from a very humble place. It's not about I know more than you or I have stuff to give you. It's not like that. I come from a place of 'if you want to check it out, feel free. I found it to be extremely beneficial'.

I offer others the opportunity to benefit from what I am enjoying.

The more I understand the experiences of my life, the more I understand the impact that I am able to make. Making a difference is my number one Core Value.

We all are influencers at whatever level we are. Our kids, partners, parents, extended family, and friends are impacted by us no matter what we do. We have influencing power and can make a difference no matter what.

So, it's very important for us to be aware of that because we are like a flower, wherever we go we spread our fragrance. The fragrance of a flower just *is*... it doesn't have to try to smell good. For us humans it's a totally different thing. As humans we get to be fully conscious and living in the present moment in order to have a positive impact in our world. This allows us to be extremely mindful of what we say or what we don't say, especially with our children.

I'm blessed to be a mother and I take that job so seriously. I am a conduit. I am like a Medium of love, attention, and understanding. Initially I am the source of everything for my children. They will benefit from a mother who is aware of her purpose, her reason for existence. If not, she will just exist.

There is a difference between existing and living. You can only turn from existing to living when you are aware of why you are alive.

Firstly, you know you are alive when you go within. It's all about going within. I always say there is no other way. That is where the real truth is... that's where the nectar is. This gives you the opportunity to see what you are really doing, how it is affecting you as well as others.

Going within is the only way out... there is no other way.

If you find you haven't been living, you can start today. Think back into your past and notice the positive impact you have made. You have had a ripple effect on so many lives just by the fact of you being alive. We all bring a different energy to the table.

Understanding that we all have a purpose and that we are all here for a reason is so important. We need each other. The first thing to do is identify that... become aware of that... and then live towards it. I want to make sure I spread the light of possibility. I just want everybody to wake up and be able to see that whatever they are seeking is already within them.

We are all here for a reason.

I'm here for a reason and you are here for a reason.

CHAPTER 5

You Are Here for a Reason

In order to really tap into that reason, you get to understand the mind. Why? Because the mind does its best to be in charge. Staying connected to who you really are... which is a soul within a human body... is what will give you the power to integrate your body, mind, and soul. We reside in our body all of our lives. Have you ever wondered who runs the body? It's the mind. The mind has many functions and capabilities, I've listed ten of them below...

Function #1 - The Mind Stores All of Our Memories: The mind is a big warehouse where all of our memories are organized and stored. Memories are labeled in the mind as good, bad, beautiful, ugly, etc. Some memories are strongly associated with events and have a date and time stamped on them. Other memories are vague, and the date and time is unclear.

Function #2 - The Mind Runs Our Body: The Mind has the perfect blueprint of what our body is like today and what it should ideally be internally and externally. This means that the mind knows our ideal state of being. It's the mechanism that signals us to rest and rejuvenate. It regulates our health. In other words, the mind maintains all of our bodily functions.

Function #3 - The Mind Enjoys Serving Us: The mind is extremely powerful. Our mind needs clear orders. Whatever we tell the mind it translates that as an order. Everything you say after "I AM..." becomes your reality. In other words, our mind likes to take orders from us... it likes to serve us. We have the benefit of being able to rewire our minds.

The mind can be tamed. It looks for commands, therefore if we aren't happy with our lives, we can give our mind some new commands. We can definitely control the mind.

Function #4 - The Mind Represses Memories: The mind represses memories that are associated with negative emotions. It brings those memories up when the time is right. They will resurface when we need to make rational choices. This is a great opportunity to release the negative emotions associated with those memories.

Our mind is very intelligent and may keep memories

repressed for our protection. When the time is not right or when the mind feels that we will not be protected, by bringing those old memories up, it will repress those memories further. So, our mind is a very intelligent being.

Function #5 – The Mind Controls & Maintains Our Perceptions: Our reality of the world is based on our perceptions. Perceptions are powerful and unique to us. All of our experiences and the stories we tell ourselves create our perceptions. They are generated, stored, and maintained in the mind. Our mind gathers all the data points that form our perceptions.

Our unconscious mind receives and transmits perceptions to our conscious mind. We can control and maintain our perceptions when we notice what they are.

Function #6 – The Mind Generates & Stores Energy: We communicate with our energy more than we communicate with words. Our energy gives the people around us a clear idea of our true being. This energy is stored in the mind, which also stores the energy we get from food, sleep, breathing, and exercise.

Our mind generates, stores, and transmits energy to the entire body. The mind determines how much energy we have.

Energy is that which connects our body and soul with the mind.

Function #7 - The Mind Maintains Instincts & Generates Habits: Instinct is a natural tendency that can be connected to what we've learned and also experienced. When we follow through and respect those instincts, our mind presents more and more of them to us thus making us super intuitive. Repetitive behaviors form habits and those habits determine the quality of our lives.

Function #8 - The Mind is Symbolic: The mind easily remembers by associating symbols. It files symbols and responds to symbols. It also files memories and the emotions associated with those memories by leveraging our five senses. This is how the mind builds strong associations with symbols.

Think about it...

Does a specific fragrance remind you of someone?

Does a sound of a specific instrument ring a bell in your head?

Do you remember the taste of your mother's hand cooked meal?

Does the touch of your partner or your kid feel extremely familiar?

Does a visual of a specific place remind you of someone?

If we need to forget something, we can do so by eliminating and repurposing that symbol for a different symbol/trigger. When we think about triggers, we think about negative triggers. There are positive triggers as well. We can use triggers to train our minds. In other words, we can use a different symbol when a certain symbol pulls us towards a negative trigger.

Function #9 - The Mind Works on the Principle of Least Effort: Truth is multidimensional and therefore every action could also have more than one meaning. Sometimes our intentions and actions are aligned and other times they are not. The mind conveniently works through this alignment or misalignment.

Mind likes to take the easy route to reach its noble goal of peace and calm. It prefers to avoid confrontations, hard work, and stepping out of its comfort zone. The mind takes the path of least resistance. It does not want to get into any conflicts or confrontations. This is why we feel held back from taking risks. Our mind does not encourage us to go in the direction that is unknown to us. It always wants to stick with the known.

Function #10 - The Mind Does Not Process Negatives: The way we speak to ourselves and others matters. Our mind does not process negatives, for example the word "don't". For a better understanding, I have included examples below.

Don't...

Don't forget to bring in the mail
(the brain hears) Forget to bring in the mail

Don't slouch.
(the brain hears) Slouch

Don't eat that
(the brain hears) Eat that

The way we speak... the emotions we convey... the language we use... makes all the difference. The way we string words together matters, because words are commands for the mind.

CHAPTER 6

Get in Touch with Your Inner Power

We cannot get in touch with our inner power until we become more mindful. In my case, I had gone from my parents, eco-chamber to my husband's eco-chamber. I was so used to that way of living and so comfortable that I never wanted anything else. When I made new friends, I would bring them home and introduce them to my husband. They would become family friends. I was so used to having family friends with my parents and then with my husband.

We knew each other's friends. We were referred to as his wife or her husband. It became very difficult for me to see myself as me. Also, in my husband's culture, they change the name of the wife. After we got married, my name was changed. It was like I had had a complete identity change in that sense. I had a new first, middle, and last name. I didn't officially change it on my documents.

I am now an American citizen and I still haven't changed it legally.

I always used my new name when I introduced myself in an attempt to completely blend in. Adaptability is actually one of my top five Strengths. There are pros and cons to our strengths.

Even though I am extremely adaptable, attempting to blend in was my con. It was very challenging to really know who I was. If you were to ask me, "Are you coming at seven for dinner tonight?" I would say, "One minute, I'll ask my husband." Everything was like that. I never thought about making my own decisions. Even if I knew we could easily arrive at 7:00 pm, I wouldn't make that decision. I never stopped to think whether or not I even wanted to go. I never thought that I could just say yes and then tell my husband the time we would be arriving. I certainly didn't think about how I could go, and he could choose not to be there. That was also an option that I never thought about.

Everything was us, not me.

So crazy!

I had a lot of awakening to do when these kinds of things happened. In hindsight, I am so grateful for the challenges that I've had in life.

With my husband's infidelity, I started to awaken for my own sake. There is a conscience that we all have and we kind of shut it down. We don't listen to it. All of a sudden, my conscience was coming out so strong for me. I've always been a believer. As I mentioned earlier, I am an extremely spiritual person. This very painful experience became the richest experience of my life.

Cut to where my husband and I are today, everything is settled. Again, it has taken a lot of work to get to where we are right now.

Instead of blaming him, cursing him, and telling others anything bad about him... I thank him. That was a wonderful victory for me. To be able to grow exponentially at a level where I could actually be thankful for somebody who changed my life is huge. It brings with it a great deal of freedom and peace. I'm not the same person. I can't even relate to the person I was at that time, being in that chamber.

The way I show up has changed. We have two boys now, and I even moved our family from one part of the US to another... from the east coast to the west coast. It's not a joke. I literally uprooted my family. We moved from Delaware to California. Once again, I moved to a place where no one knew me. This time I wasn't working at the same company as my husband. This alone made a huge difference for me.

I found my own identity.

We now have different friends and I only bring them home if I want to... so conceptually they know I have a husband, they might not have met him yet. This time I made sure there was not too much blending going on. I now have a very different approach towards life.

I have grown leaps and bounds from what and who I was before, and so has my husband. We now consciously work on our relationship every day and have created a positive, thriving environment for our kids.

Right now, I feel rich. I don't know if there is any other word that I can share to describe the outcome of all I have been through. I have come to learn one thing for sure.

No matter what experiences we go through, we get to grow through those experiences. That's where the success lies, that's where we find our golden nuggets. Even if you go through something *crying*, you will stop crying at some point.

You can grow through something and actually build something beautiful out of it one day. That's the path I chose. This is why I'm writing this book and have started a coaching practice.

Having gone from being nobody to feeling like I am somebody of value and seeing my uniqueness, I know others can as well. There are so many people going through infidelity issues and so many other situations like mine.

My situation was not that unique.

The way I dealt with it was definitely unique, because it was me.

This book is about my holistic growth, and the blossoming of my unique nature.

This whole experience, all of the events and growth I went through, led to where I am today. Until writing this book, I had not shared this part of my story with anybody.

I already have many social media followers, just from sharing the benefits of what my life has brought me. So, imagine when they read this book and then combine the outcomes with my story. It will be crazy.

CHAPTER 7

Problems Are in the Mind

Problems are in the mind. Our limiting beliefs are the only limiting factors in life. If we have not achieved whatever we want to achieve so far in our lives, it's just because we believe we are not able to do so. Now that I know who I am and believe in myself, the door to all possibilities has opened up for me. It's fun to be me and live life right now. I feel so alive.

I'm grateful for every single day. Each day comes with umpteen million possibilities. Whatever I want to make it through I will. That's what I believe and that's what is evident to all of the people all around me. I know my kids feel it as well.

I want to *radiate* the importance of being alive. That's how I want to come across, and that's how I am living life these days. I own the fact that my problems are in my mind. If there is anything that is blocking me from doing what I want to do, it is because I am limiting myself in my mind. When I am not letting go of things, I am creating a rigid mindset. It's only human to be like that so I'm not saying I'm superhuman.

We all deal with limiting beliefs: fear, anger, guilt, shame, etc. These are all emotions. Sometimes they serve us and sometimes they don't. The good news is that our limiting beliefs can be changed.

Love and joy are really important for me. Peace is my ultimate state of BEing, where everything settles down. That's the vibration I enjoy the most.

As divine beings, our core state is that of being calm. Whatever we believe about our God, energy, a higher power, whatever we believe in that is all loving and beautiful, it puts us into a space of acceptance.

When we are struggling emotionally, it's kind of like water that is starting to boil. It's difficult to get to the core state of peace and it's easy to become worried.

Water is always flowing very naturally.

If you turn on the gas water will start to boil. If you put a container of water in the freezer it will harden. Either way, it's still the same water, it's just showing up in a different form. When you find yourself going into frustration and moving towards anger, all you have to do is turn off the gas. In other words, pull yourself away from the things that are creating those emotions.

Find the source and pull away from it. Once you pull away, that's the only act you have to do.

When you turn the gas off, water comes to its natural temperature all by itself. When it is in the refrigerator or in the freezer, all you have to do is just pull it away from there as well. If you are living your life in lala land, everything seems fine. You are actually in a frozen, numbed out state. *You don't have to do something different* to be your natural self. *You just have to stop doing things that take you away* from your natural state.

Our mind is what constructs our reality. If my mind is telling me that someone is a good person, then that's my reality. If my mind is saying no that person can't be trusted, then that's what I will believe. It has nothing to do with who the other person truly is.

Our minds interpret what we like or who we like, and what we don't like or who we don't like. There are multiple layers in the mind. I get very deep into that in my coaching. I dig deeper with my clients to figure out why they are believing certain things. What is the lens they are seeing life through? If they are wearing glasses that have red lenses, the whole world will appear as red to them.

We create more clarity when we are able to change our lens. As co-creators of our world, we attract possibility into reality and watch it actually come to fruition just with the power of our minds. It's so important to be aware of that fact. This is why I say create responsibly.

Make sure you are clear about what you want to create. If you are considering a one-thousand square foot house, that's most likely what will manifest. Pay attention to the specifics of what you are thinking about, in other words, what you are co creating with God, the Universe or whatever higher power you believe in. Be very, very conscious of what it is that you want to create.

Everything starts with the wanting. Then the decision to do the work.

A. You want it.

B. You are willing to put in the work.

These are the prerequisites for anything that you want to accomplish in life. If you want to be happy and successful in life, there are two simple things to do.

Always avoid saying "Always"

Never say "Never"

Why?

Because you never know all-the-ways and Never is always changing.

CHAPTER 8

Create Responsibly

I love the word ACTION because it trumps all great intentions. I take the time to be introspective, reminiscent, and do the groundwork for full blown action in all the areas of deep interest to me.

Great things happen when we take action and implement. This is why I'm a big fan of implementing what I have learned. This way I can create responsibly in the world. I am fortunate to be able to teach mindfulness and implementation to people across the world. I continue to do the same for myself.

Continuous action is in the present tense for me. Not in the past or in the future - right now in the present is where I ACT.

How about you? Do you operate in the NOW?

Our actions are dictated by our emotions. The emotion you can easily feel most of the time is your natural core state. Any emotion that you cannot maintain long term is a temporary state and not your core state.

Ask yourself if any of these emotions are possible for you to feel MOST of THE TIME...

Hatred

Anger

Sadness

Love

Happiness

Peaceful

Many people confuse their temporary state with their core state and end up leading a miserable life. The choice is YOURS - Always remember to create responsibly, which means understand your emotions.

We experience conflict when our emotions conflict with others. For example, *what I inaccurately think about you* and *what you inaccurately think about me* leads to conflict.

Varying thoughts and interpretations that arise in our minds, travel to our hearts, and show up in our actions. It's a great idea to nip conflict in the bud. For that we need to understand where conflicts start.

Instead of building assumptions it is better to discuss and clarify them.

My goal is to empower people to replace their negative emotions as they do not serve anyone and cause more harm than good.

These negative emotions might be caused by events, experiences, and/or other people. I am wise enough to know that we cannot eliminate anything from our lives without leaving a void. We get to replace it with something else. For example...

Hatred - to - Acceptance

Sadness - to - Hope

Fear - to - Courage, Confidence, Belief

Anger - to – Forgiveness

Hurt - to - Love

With every experience and with every person we encounter in life, there are some emotions associated with them. When an experience is over or when a person has left, we feel a void. The question is *how will we fill that void*? We have a choice... we can fill it with feelings of pain, hurt, resentment, etc. or with something positive, something that is going to serve us.

Are you experiencing a void in your life? If so, what is it?

What do you choose to replace it with?

Radical self-awareness is understanding that YOU HAVE A CHOICE - every step of the way - for everything in your life. In other words, you have a choice to become fully aware and conscious about everything you accept, as well as reject.

Being congruent within your mind, body, and soul is a result of the yes/no choices you make that fill you with confidence and not fear.

Fully understanding that when you're saying "yes" to something, you're automatically saying "no" to everything else.

Can this awareness be cultivated? YES!

How? By forming consistent habits.

When you have clarity and a positive mindset, you rise above the "what ifs" that hold you back. Your confidence rises and therefore your results improve drastically!

Single most cause of our...

Pain is *Entitlement*

Happiness is *Responsibility*

Health is *Food & Exercise*

Growth is *Persistence*

Success is *Gratitude*

When you let go of negative emotions, are you really letting them go completely or are you letting them be like in a parking lot?

When we let something go completely it goes away and when we let something be it stays. However simple and basic this sounds, we often forget that when we let negative emotions such as anger, hatred, resentment, hurt, jealousy and so on just be... they end up BEing around us and within us continuing to cause us harm.

Value your peace enough to let the negativity go. The best thing is that we have the power to let them go at any time!

How do you deal with negative emotions?

As humans we have the privilege to accept others for who they are... be kind to others no matter what... and spread love, inclusion, and belongingness. We unite with others on World Unity Day by celebrating acceptance, love, kindness, inclusion, non-judgment, and so on.

Why limit celebrating to one day a year? Let's celebrate every day!

CHAPTER 9
Find Yourself Within

When you start *a journey within* the first question is "Why me?" That's an answer that nobody can give you. In order to understand what is going on you get to meditate, and the answer will be unveiled. It will all open up to you in that realm.

When I started my journey within, I realized that I had so many strengths. Before that I was always thinking, 'Oh, I'm not so smart and what do I have to give?'

I eventually lost my sense of value and worth.

When everything in my life started to fall apart, I asked myself, 'Am I a nobody now? Does anybody even see me?' So, to gain my visibility back, I had to slow down and really see myself. I needed to listen to myself. I started to spend long moments in front of the mirror just looking at me and taking in every fine detail. Then

I started talking to myself, the one in the mirror, and saying kind things. I started to fall in love with my own self for the very first time. Imagine living in this particular body for so many years and not really knowing her.

So that's where it started for me. As I stepped into my true self I was like, 'Okay, you can't take this person lightly at all. She's the real deal.' As I learned to love myself more and more, I couldn't help but share *me* authentically with others. When you have enough and when you know enough, you can't help but share.

Knowing my true self was extremely important for me.

Knowing true self is about knowing who you are at a spiritual level and at the very practical level. This helped me to understand my limitations.

Understanding my weaknesses and my strengths was extremely important for me to grow.

We have full potential. When I say that to myself or others, I am talking about endless possibilities. There are no caps, no lids on our jars, no glass ceilings. We are divine beings. Just by the very nature of that alchemy itself, we have ultimate possibilities available to us. We can bring about whatever our minds decide. I have experienced that in life. Our limiting beliefs are the only caps. As we get rid of those beliefs the lids keep opening and we are no longer feeling trapped.

For me, I had never thought that I could get a master's degree. I had never thought I could work in a number one marketing agency. I had never thought I could come to this foreign country, make a life, build a dream house or write this book.

Living our full potential only comes from wanting to live it. That is very important. Once we have that we get to remind ourselves that we have the choice to up level ourselves.

We get a new phone because we want the most upgraded version out there. How about upgrading your own self to the latest and greatest upgrade possible in any given moment?

Cell phone upgrades will keep on coming. So, keep on upgrading yourself. I want to be the best version I can be of myself. That's how we continuously evolve. Right? So that's what I mean when I say, "There's no limit to the way you can evolve".

Instead of saying, "I will do my best today" say "I did my best today." In other words, just do it and reflect that you did your best with what you had that day.

Growing is the most selfless thing we can do, which is contrary to popular belief. When we take care of our own self it comes to be the most beneficial for everyone around us. When we allow this blossoming, everyone sees the beauty and enjoys its fragrance.

There are some people who will become jealous and leave and that's okay. They are finding their own way through this journey called life.

The Lotus flower is a symbol of that and why I chose it to be part of my logo. Flowers attract bees and that's where the honey is so just follow those bees and connect with others.

CHAPTER 10

Connect with It

Connecting with your True self allows you to heal so you can connect with others. Our wounds become fertilizer for our growth. The best part about my story and why I feel so rich is because I was down to the ashes. I went from not feeling visible at all to becoming the most visible person in my mind.

I love movies, I am the hero of my own movie. We all are. I am the hero of my movie and you are the hero of your movie. I play a supporting cast in yours and you play a supporting cast in mine. When we understand this... it opens us up to a whole new realm.

While I was growing up if I asked my mom what she wanted she would say, "Whatever you want." I was like, Mom, what about you?

I just love my mom to death and the way she was being

was coming from a good place, that's just how she had always lived. It makes me so happy to watch my mom living life for herself now. She's doing what she wants to do for herself. It's just beautiful to see her living this way.

What is it that you want to learn about in life? Going within is how to connect with your True self. The best time to go within is when you don't have anywhere else to go. The door is wide open at that time. That's the door I took in my life and that's when all the magic happened.

When you go inside you are able to go over your past experiences and see what they have taught you. This gives you the opportunity to see and think about your patterns of behavior. It's also a great time to consider the people that you are surrounding yourself with. You can ask yourself questions like: 'What is the good I have done so far? What is the bad that I have done so far?'

Looking within is a time of introspection. It's a way to look in the rearview mirror and see the distance you've already covered. This will give you a baseline for moving forward. It will also help you see your strengths.

The distance you have covered and the challenges you have overcome, will give you a sense of confidence as you navigate further on in life.

Experiencing Highs and Lows

Whenever you are at the lowest of low, that's not where you've always been. Right? You have also experienced highs. Recalling the highs will bring you back up. In order to avoid the lowest low, you have to go to the highest high possible. When I say the lowest low, for example, I don't want to feel invisible or like I'm a nobody.

Introspection will help you to keep on building your energy up, up, up. This is what *continuous life of evolution* is all about. The journey of evolution is where you elevate yourself so high, that the lowest low is not even visible for you anymore. You can't get there even if you tried.

CHAPTER 11

Shine from that Place

The way to shine as your True self is to befriend your inner being and stay loyal to it at all times. It's also about looking at *who we can become.* It is a journey of realizing our complete potential and tapping into it in order to live a more fulfilled and happy life.

The most important person you're going to be surrounded by at all times is YOU! Hence it is very important to focus on yourself. In other words, become self-aware. Being self-aware is not selfish. Self-aware people have a few traits that are so distinct that they have a completely different perspective on life.

Self-awareness is a prerequisite to becoming a true giver. Why? You can only give what you have, what you can create, and what you know you have in ample supply. When the joy of giving is bigger than keeping it for yourself, you will know the true joy of giving.

Self-aware leaders are the greatest givers. They are comfortable in their own skin and super aware of what they can bring to the table. This is why they have no issues in sharing. They believe that sharing is caring.

Self-aware leaders give joy, hope, positivity, and love in ample quantities. This is why they automatically become our idols and role models.

The ultimate wish of every individual is to be understood by others. The ultimate skill every individual would like to possess is the ability to understand others.

Self-awareness bridges the gap between understanding ourselves fully and...

Communicating effectively

Expressing openly

Relating with others authentically

How self-aware are you?

Self-awareness is a very foundational leadership skill. We talk about Intelligence Quotient (I.Q.) and Emotional Quotient (E.Q.), do we really know our Awareness Quotient (A.Q.)?

What does that even mean?

The understanding and combination of our strengths and weaknesses give us our A.Q. score, which reflects our level of self-awareness.

Awareness is about understanding who we are and what is within us. If we are not aware of who we are, how can we help someone else understand us? If we do understand ourselves and someone says they don't understand us, most likely they don't understand themselves.

Self-awareness is the fuel that will make the ride to success much smoother in the journey of life. Self-awareness is fundamental in life for your success.

Your Awareness Quotient = Your Success Quotient

Heightened self-awareness increases clarity and gives you greater control over your thoughts, actions, and feelings. You become more responsible in other words you exhibit more responsible behavior. This increases your confidence. You will have less dependencies, fewer false expectations, and less regrets. You will also be able to take more action and experience more wins with greater success.

What role has self-awareness played in your growth?

As a transformation coach, I get to work with a lot of entrepreneurs and leaders who are willing to tap into their complete potential and live a life of happiness and fulfillment.

Happiness

The shortest route to happiness lies between our head and our heart. The longest route to happiness is borrowing temporary moments of pleasure and gratification from others before finding your own. You can find your own happiness today. Go within. Go to the source.

Responsibility

The single most important reason for happiness is taking responsibility. The single most important reason for pain is feeling entitled. The single most important purpose of my life is to help my clients shift from a blaming mindset to the one that takes ownership and responsibility for everything, every time! Taking responsibility does not mean being responsible for the outcome, it means sincerely and consciously doing everything in your power to improve any situation with highest integrity.

How? By starting with radical self-awareness and working your way through self-realization.

This includes strategies, consistent action, and serious breakthroughs.

Are you ready for the transformation?

In this uncertain world, the only thing you can be certain of is your-SELF! You can only be certain about the things that are within your control.

What are the things you CAN control? Well, something that you fully own.

What is it that you fully own? YOUR mind. YOUR thoughts. YOUR actions.

Challenges

Challenges are a small part of life and therefore need to be treated as such. When our challenges take control and start ruling our minds, that's when we start getting out-of-sync. We start becoming *who we are not* as our negative limiting beliefs are formed. When our view of the world changes... we feel broken, stuck, and lost.

Overcoming Challenges - Dealing with Problems, Feelings & Actions

Problems - Avoid over thinking them

Feelings - Avoid over feeling them

Actions - Avoid over doing them

When we stop overthinking, over feeling, and over doing things - our problems, feelings, and actions don't get the better of us. That doesn't happen overnight!

Consistency is the key here and in order to keep that momentum going, we need someone who can be our cheerleader. I have the utmost honor of being that person for many and I take that responsibility very seriously.

Let's overcome our challenges and control what we *can* control.

How? Shine a lot more. Laugh a lot more. Succeed a lot more.

Success

SUCCESS is what we all chase. What is success? How do we achieve it? If financial success was the only measure of success in life, the world's richest would be the worlds' HAPPIEST. If physical fitness was the only measure of success in life, the world's fittest would be the worlds' HAPPIEST. If social wealth (fame, popularity) was the only measure of success, the world's most famous would be the worlds' HAPPIEST.

HAPPINESS is the wealth that is not dependent on financial, physical or social success. It is dependent on mental and spiritual success. Putting my energy where it matters the most is what I love doing!

We all have our definitions of success, however, sometimes success in one dimension of life can take us off balance from several other key dimensions. Here are a few questions you can ask yourself after you work hard and succeed at getting a promotion at work...

Were you simultaneously also successful at keeping your family happy?

Were you successful at staying healthy?

Were you growing personally?

The 3 things you need to be mindful of when it comes to success...

Clarity in your mind is number one.

Innocence in your heart is number two.

Dexterity in your actions is number three.

Success Mantra: "I have clarity in my mind, innocence in my heart, and dexterity in my actions."

What does success mean to you? What is your success mantra?

CHAPTER 12

You Are Here to Illuminate

When we focus on our health, we increase our capacity to shine. This allows us to succeed in a way that feels good and decreases our pain. You cannot enjoy your wealth without your health.

I always share a gentle reminder with my clients and followers which is to focus on their health. When you're healthy - you can find a million ways to be wealthy - that's what I tell them. I also teach them the importance of *me-time* and empower them to figure out how to make it their primary focus in life. Each week they create a list of things that will allow them to become successful, feel accomplished, and earn money as well as respect.

Self-aware people are very focused on their health. When they hear the word health they don't just think about their physical health. They understand the mind-body-soul connection and how that connection affects their health and the health of others. They also know that true success depends on how healthy, self-reliant, and capable one is. Therefore, they tend to take care of their holistic wellbeing by forming good habits and prioritizing their self-care time daily.

As humans we are interdependent... so we are dependent on each other for our wellness. This is called holistic well-being. It's about staying fit physically, mentally, emotionally, and spiritually... as well as being aware of how we can help others do the same. This is a beautiful gift of self-awareness.

Another key trait of a self-aware person is that they express themselves openly. This allows them to live lightly and express themselves fully. They do not hold back, worry about any judgments or calculate their emotions. They are themselves and empower others around them to do the same.

Self-expression helps to build trust and foster deep connection. Self-aware people tend to be very expressive. They often hug others, smile, and are extremely open about their feelings. In other words, they don't hold back and encourage others to do the same. Most importantly they understand the differences in others, so they know not everyone wants a hug.

Not all self-aware leaders are extroverts, actually introverts and highly sensitive people (HSPs) tend to be the most self-aware, however they aren't always recognized as leaders.

Self-Care

As leaders it's important to focus on self-care. I take frequent breaks from social media. I refrain from creating and posting content to reflect on how far I have come, where I am headed, and how I can fine tune my messaging in order to connect with my audience more effectively.

Those mental breaks are very refreshing. As a result, my mind begins to brew ideas and thoughts on how much I have to say and how wonderfully I can say it.

Self-introspection is key for anyone that is wanting to up level in life. Meditation is the path that takes us within. I'm overwhelmed by the magic that unfolds when we tap into the source - our core!

Give it a try!

Create Holistic Wealth

Money matters a whole lot and yet money is not the only thing that matters. There are eight different types of wealth. Each of them is equally important. Properly attending to them empowers us to prosper, succeed, and derive a sense of fulfillment.

Time Wealth

We can't say for sure how much time we have before we die. When we share this limited precious resource with someone, it should be a transaction worth having with full awareness and conscious decisioning. We cannot earn this wealth back, nor can we generate more of it hence it is the most precious of all.

Health Wealth

Health is wealth because to earn material wealth, we will need to be in healthy condition physically, mentally, emotionally, psychologically, and so on. All of these different dimensions of our being are included in our health and wellness wealth. When we are healthy, we are best positioned to not only become wealthy but also enjoy that wealth.

Financial Wealth

Money is the common language everyone in the world speaks. We are all mentally wired to earn money as a source of living, because the value of money and its importance in our life has been passed on to us genealogically. Money is the tangible form of wealth that we can earn, multiply, and share. It gives us a sense of security because it empowers us to transact with others in return for a valuable product or service.

Relationship (Family / Friends) Wealth

This is perhaps one of the wealths that we take for granted. We all know that having friends and family is a blessing, we often do not fully realize their value until we lose them. Having someone around us who supports us and cheers for us is priceless. Wealthy are those that have such people in their life, around them at all times.

Spiritual Wealth

Attending the needs of the soul is one of the most gratifying experiences in life. Wealthy are those who spend time in silence, do the inner work, and tend to their soul. Spiritual and mental wellbeing is the cornerstone of a successful life and is often the foundation on which all other riches lie.

Business / Profession Wealth

The work that we do brings us more than just money. Recognition is a big motivator. Job satisfaction, rewards, empowerment, confidence, etc. are all instrumental in our overall success professionally. When we have something to do, we have nothing to worry about. Doing meaningful work and working towards a purpose greater than ourselves is a great form of wealth.

Creative Wealth

Creativity is a natural phenomenon. It is the power of the brain that requires continuous nudges and freedom of expression. When we become curious and want to learn more, we grow and expose ourselves to a world of possibilities. Expressing ourselves creatively is a wealth we must and can afford.

Experience Wealth

The luxuries we enjoy in life and the experiences we have are a special kind of wealth. Experience wealth isn't just about money. The time we spend in nature is definitely a big part of experience wealth. There are many experiences we can enjoy without including money.

Cuddling on the couch with our kids, having a picnic with our spouse, visiting local sites, enjoying a free concert in the park, etc. These are just a few examples of how experience wealth makes us richer and able to live more abundant lives.

Gratitude

To become great in life... be grateful. Leaders are grateful. Self-aware leaders are ALWAYS grateful, even during the time of adversity. Gratitude is something that they totally believe in, it's an emotion that they feel every single day. They have the ability to count their blessings by seeing the positive in everything and every situation.

They are thankful for everything they are experiencing in life and know they can overcome and grow from any negative experience. Their self-awareness shows them that there's something good hidden in everything.

Similarly, with every step towards success, self-aware leaders recognize the contributions of their team members. They are well aware of the fact that success is a team effort. Counting your blessings and being grateful every day is a wonderful trait of self-awareness.

Are you comfortable in claiming that you're ALWAYS grateful?

Your level of gratitude...

Introduces your character

Showcases your attitude

Defines your altitude

Determines your level of success in life

Is directly proportional to your happiness in life

We cannot be deeply grateful unless we are fully self-aware.

BLOSSOM INTO YOUR UNIQUE SELF

Through my life experiences,
I learned the importance of becoming
my own cheerleader.
I became financially independent.
I also became emotionally independent.
Understanding the importance of mindset, journaling,
and meditation got me into just the right garden for
me to bloom.

*Use the following section to deepen your
self-awareness!*

Mindset

Are you feeling good about who you are? Are you feeling good about where you are in life? If so, is this feeling increasing each day?

When we start appreciating the good things that are happening, we finally start seeing them as a blessing that we deserve. This change in attitude will help us to feel more confident and hopeful.

As our emotional health gets more and more robust, our physical health will improve as well. These two aspects of our lives are more interconnected than we realize.

When was the last time you checked in with yourself?

Failure

We all experience challenges and failures. Every inspiring success has been reached by walking innumerable steps of failure. Our personalities are a mix of our abilities, as well as our inabilities.

The key ingredients to turn every *Back Story* into a *Victory Story* are...

Courage
Optimism

Self-belief

Action

Note to Self: Failures become stepping-stones to success only for those who do not GIVE UP!

Do you know how to turn your failures into stepping-stones?

Fear

Fear is an emotion that is experienced by all human beings. It comes from a belief that is fully powered by our minds. This is why fear comes in varying degrees and how deeply it affects each one of us. Our fear is only as real and as strong as we decide we want it to be. What we believe, we achieve.

Self-aware leaders experience fear and they face it head on. In other words, they work on and through their fears and limiting beliefs. They keep going and do not let the fear stop them.

Raising our self-belief keeps fear from overpowering our thoughts, actions, and reactions. When we are in control and when we make sure that we are greater than the fear we are experiencing, then we can rise up, face the situation, and come out as a winner.

Self-aware leaders are extremely aware of this fact and

they face fear head on. They are not afraid of any of their limiting beliefs or shortcomings. They work on rising above all of them.

How do you deal with fear?

Magic

A miracle feels magical, and MAGIC is the keyword these days. Everyone is hoping for a miracle. Everyone is expecting one. Magic can happen all day every day, not just in December.

When our thoughts are aligned with our emotions - magic happens.

When our emotions are aligned with our actions - magic happens.

When our actions are aligned with our vision - magic happens.

These alignments can happen every day and they are not time sensitive. They are intention and awareness sensitive. Make the most out of your life every single day. It's a gift. Maximize your potential by aligning the above and witness the magic unfolding in your life every single day.

When your Sole purpose in life is aligned with your Soul's purpose... MAGIC happens!

Going Within

The best time to go within is when you don't have anywhere else to go. The door is wide open at that time. That's the door I took in my life and that's when all the magic happened. When you go inside you are able to go back through your past experiences and see what those experiences have taught you. The learnings from that review will enrich your future experiences.

Connection

In order to connect with others, we need to be able to connect with ourselves first. Surround yourself with people who you admire. Find a common ground between yourself and them. This will take going within and doing some more self-exploration.

The adage "Keep good company" is a reminder, more than a message.

Surround Yourself With "Yay" Sayers

Rather than surrounding yourself with naysayers, surround yourself with "Yay" sayers.

Having the right kind of people around you is just as important if not more, than having the right amount of sugar in your coffee.

Just as too much sugar, despite its wonderful, sweet taste is harmful - so are some of the people in our lives. Surrounding ourselves with people who complement our skills is often more important than surrounding ourselves with the ones who compliment, our looks or our clothing.

The secret to my success has been consciously choosing the people I surround myself with.

Presence

Being present with someone is the best *present* you can give them. It's also a gift you give yourself. We learn more when we are fully present. This is a powerful ingredient for the magic that allows us to deeply connect with ourselves and others. Presence is giving someone your full and undivided attention, which makes everyone feel good.

Give the gift of your presence to someone everyday....

In every conversation

In every interaction

In every action

Show them that you care, show them that you are listening, and tell them that they matter.

People want to feel...

Valued

Cared for

Important

Your presence, really seeing them and listening to them, will make them feel all of the above.

Conversational Triggers

When was the last time that you felt fired up and energized after talking with somebody? I believe it is important to surround ourselves with people who are not like us. The ones who complement our energies and efficiencies. Someone who talks to us about things we don't typically think about. This is a person who can trigger us in a way we don't normally get triggered.

Noticing our triggers helps us to evolve and grow. These types of conversations always brighten my day. I now have the confidence to look at things that I am not consciously aware of about myself, like how I am wired. There are things that are natural to me that I don't even see without having conversations with others. For instance, a strength that I viewed as a weakness. We will never know unless we join the conversation.

Simplicity

Simplicity to me is the foundational step to effective communication. Self-aware leaders believe in simplicity. They tend to stay as far away from complexity as possible because they like to save time. Self-aware leaders know that complexity wastes a great deal of time. They speak simply, so they can live lightly.

The benefits of simplicity are endless...

Saves time and energy

Saves money

Saves burn out and redundant work

Brings in clarity and therefore efficiency

Makes everything we do joyful

What does simplicity mean to you?

How does it make your life better?

The best compliment I've ever gotten is that I talk simply and it's easy for others to understand what I'm trying to express. When we are busy attempting to understand what the complex situation is... we often lose out on the fun that simplicity could bring and how fast we could have arrived at a solution.

Smiles

Smiles are contagious! I like smiling and being surrounded by people who smile. The most attractive person for me is not the one who wears lots of makeup. It's the one who wears a smile that never wears off.

Do you know someone who smiles often and is always happy? Someone who makes sure to get back to that happy state again and again. When somebody smiles, they are just making sure that none of their problems, none of their challenges are bigger than who they are. They have the self-belief that they are greater than the problem itself. No problem is permanent in nature and each problem is solvable. Smiling and being joyful is a beautiful trait of self-aware leaders.

How often do you smile?

Leadership

Leadership is the art of achieving collective success by knowing what NOT to do, think or say. I empower leaders to find their voice, mojo, and sanity. A good leader LISTENS - to what is being said and what is NOT being said. A good leader OBSERVES - what his or her team does and what they do NOT do. A good leader KNOWS - the right time to speak up and the right time to remain SILENT.

So, it's not always what a leader does that shows us their personality and caliber, it's also what they Do NOT do that indicates their character. When I coach leaders, we dive deep into what they need to STOP doing, before we work on the things they can start doing, going forward.

Truly Lead

L - Listen to Learn: This way you will understand what others are saying.

E - Exemplify Your Message: Be true to who you are, walk your talk.

A - Appreciate: Appreciation is about acknowledging others.

D - Develop Others: You can be a gateway for people to grow and thrive or you can block their development.

Leading Others

You must ensure that you L.E.A.D yourself first. Until you do, you will not have the ability, power, and experience to work with others and help them grow. When I work with my clients, we review their sphere of influence. In other words, we look at how and where they are influencing others.

Lead yourself first...

L - Listen to your gut/inner voice

E - Energize yourself everyday

A - Accept yourself fully and completely

D - Discover your own potential

How do you L.E.A.D. yourself?

Habits

A human being is only as evolved as his or her habits. Let me break this down a bit for you. Humans have ALWAYS had the power of choice. We exercise the right to choose consciously or unconsciously at every stage in life.

Consistently chosen actions become habits. These habits are then stored as *preferences* in our subconscious mind. When we repeatedly perform those actions consciously or in auto-mode those preferences become deeply embedded into our subconscious and become habits. If our habits are good... they can accelerate our growth and if they are bad... they negatively impact our lives across all dimensions.

To overcome our deeply rooted negative habits, we get to become aware of them. This is part of what it means to be mindful. We get to consciously and consistently unlearn them. This allows us to make better choices. In order to overlook the challenges of changing a habit, focus on the outcomes you'd like to see or have.

Self-aware leaders are very mindful and courageous when it comes to noticing their habits. They understand that we can't just quit a bad habit, we must replace it with a better one. Having habits that build us up and positively affect our physical, mental, emotional, and spiritual well-being are habits worth having.

Cultivating good habits requires...

Complete Acceptance

Mindful Replacements

Consistent Practice

Daily Accountability

What Does It Take to E.V.O.L.V.E. Into A Self-Aware Leader?

E - Everyday Accountability

V - Visualizing a better version of life

O - Tapping into the origin (the root cause)

L- Leaving old habits and replacing them with new ones (very important)

V - Verification and consistency checks

E - Establishing mindfulness as a practice

What is the best habit you have seen in an inspiring, self-aware leader? What habits are you forming to become a better leader?

Balance

Balance is often not easy to achieve. That's because nothing is ever perfectly balanced. When we achieve a more balanced life, we realize that balance is our goldmine. This way we can focus on all the things that are important to us in life. Those things that tap into our creativity. We can lead a fulfilled life across all dimensions: personal, professional, social, psychological, etc. Self-aware leaders understand the importance of balance.

Benefits of leading a balanced life..

No burn out

No stress

No anxiety

More joy

More creativity

More success

What does living-a-balanced-life mean to you?

Dreaming

Dreaming is the art of visualizing and believing an event has already occurred. Your dreams could be a preview to your upcoming reality. Self-aware leaders are fully aware of their capabilities. They know when to tap into other people's strengths with the goal of achieving the vision in their mind.

There is no one-upmanship when it comes to self-aware leaders. They know that in order to achieve a vision, many men and women must join them.

Self-aware leaders are dreamers and achievers!

What is the dream you're currently manifesting into reality?

Forgiveness

Your ability to forgive others is directly proportional to your ability to forgive yourself. Read that again. When you become radically self-aware, you realize a few things...

A. No one is perfect

B. Basically no one is good

C. No one is only filled with flaws without any good hidden in them

D. Basically no one is bad

Nothing in this world is completely good or completely bad. In other words, there's no black or white. This combination makes the color grey. I believe this world has eight billion shades of grey.

Self-aware leaders understand the grey, and that is why they easily forgive themselves and others. They believe in moving on and not staying stuck in the low energy of blame and hurt. There are learnings from every situation we face.

Have you forgiven yourself and others for everything?

As your level of awareness increases in life, so will your ability to forgive others. The more we become aware of our own shortcomings and our strengths, the more we are able to forgive people for their shortcomings. Self-aware leaders focus on the good in others and forgive the unpleasant. The first thing they do is forgive themselves. We can't forgive others if we haven't forgiven ourselves.

Kindness

The self-aware leader is always very kind. Kindness is a great measure to understand how aware a person is because it is an understanding of our differences with acceptance. This gives us the strength to be kind. When we are accepting of each other's differences, we can easily coexist together and it's easy to be kind.

Kindness is one of the most important traits of a self-aware leader. Why? Because when you have worked on yourself you become aware of who you were, who you are, and who you can become. Kindness means that the leader has done their inner work to accept themselves and others.

Do you believe that kindness is a measure of strength?

Acceptance

The very first step to achieving success in life is acceptance. The sooner we accept... the faster we can resolve, move on, and succeed. I'm talking about the acceptance of every situation, person, and event in life.

Self-aware leaders know this and therefore accept everyone as they are... including themselves. They celebrate other people's points of view because it encourages them to look at things from a different perspective. It encourages them to have a dialogue from a place of curiosity that helps them to grow as an individual. Accepting people *as they are*, is the mantra of the self-aware leader.

What are your thoughts on acceptance?

Do you struggle to accept yourself?

Do you accept the differences of other people?

Approachability

Before working on your leadership ability, work on your approachability. One of the most attractive traits in a leader is APPROACHABILITY. If someone cannot talk to you, how can they ever connect with you? When someone cannot connect with you, how can you lead or inspire them? I believe in walking the talk. That's why I invite my 46K+ followers, my LinkedIn family, to reach out and ask me anything! I do my best to provide the best guidance possible.

Stress

In our truest state of being, we are all divine souls. We are all pure, loving, and peaceful human beings by nature. This is our innate state. As we go through life and its challenges, our peaceful nature gets disturbed. Our happiness quotient starts diminishing and love starts to fade.

We don't stop being an emotional and sensitive person when we are at work and at the same time, we don't stop being a leader and strategic thinker when we are at home. Both of these roles are intertwined and inseparable. We are always the same person... the same mind, body, and soul.

Even though our actions may differ at home vs. work, our inner environment stays the same. The things that bother us and stress us out at work will continue to bother us when we are at home. Things that affect our mental state, due to personal reasons, will bother us at work as well. Stress impacts our personal and professional life, because it impacts our minds.

Power

One of the most misunderstood words in history is Power. When you use your power responsibly it becomes your Superpower.

As soon as we say the word POWER, we think about...

Entitlement

Ability

Control

Dominance of People, Places, Things, Situations, etc.

Personally - I love the word Power - it reminds me of...

Capability

Confidence

Growth

Freedom

Responsibility

When we crave for power, we are truly craving for attention and recognition. You might even think this attention and recognition will come from money alone.

The truth is power comes from...

The spirit of joy within you

Your ability to serve others

Your self-belief and confidence

Your inner strength

Your self-awareness

As I look back, I can see the power of my life. By writing this book and revealing my story, I opened up a place within me to receive a completely, fulfilling life.

What does the word Power mean to you?

Think about this and meditate on it: "Where do I get my power?"

Strengths

Leadership is doing what you're good at and becoming the best at it. The benefit of having awareness about our strengths is that we can easily maximize on what it is that...

We enjoy doing

We are good at

We can share with others to inspire them

Self-aware leaders focus on their strengths and become masters of their domain / industry. They master that one thing that is their top strength.

What is your top strength?

NOTE FROM THE AUTHOR

I had been thinking of creating and sharing content on social media since 2017. I did not do so until mid-2018. That wasn't because I didn't have anything to say. It was because I was very conscious of wanting to come across as intelligent and in control of my life and my mind.

I was unknowingly dealing with a lot of anxiety.

Why?

Because we feel the world is judging us, we decide we have to live up to the expectations and standards a society has set up for us. Right? After all, that's when we will be considered as thought leaders isn't it?

Guess what?!?
This couldn't be further from the truth.

It's not about the achievement as much it is about the struggle and the juggle.

It is not about being a thought leader as much it is about being relatable.

It is not about being intelligent as much it is about learning and journaling.

It is not about being successful as much it is about being vulnerable.

It is not about Return On Investment as much as it is about Rise Of Intellect.

Believing in ourselves, being open, humble, and hungry to learn... are the key things we need to succeed in anything we do.

Others may judge you. That's their problem, not yours!

**If we dare to be path breakers,
we can become path pavers for many.**

**When you do good for yourself,
you become successful.**

**When you do good for others,
you become peaceful.**

**When you do good WITH others,
you become powerful.**

RESOURCE ARTICLES

I've included some of my articles as an extra bonus. I trust you will enjoy them as much as I enjoyed writing them.

Wealth That Makes You Prosperous

It is widely believed that wealth equates to material richness. The one that has more money is better off than the one who does not. Material wealth (being monetarily rich) is a global measure to determine the affluence a person, state or a country enjoys. There is also a disparity in wealth distribution across the globe?

Wealth is not just money as we understand it. Money is a mere means to the destination. When someone yearns for money, they are essentially seeking something that money can buy to make them happy. Similarly, when someone earns money, they are merely earning the capability to buy something that can give them happiness. Once this concept is clear in our minds, we can be open to understand the difference between being monetarily rich vs. wealthy.

There are 8 different types of wealth that bring us holistic happiness, prosperity, and joy in life.

#1 - Time Wealth

The resource of time is the most critical of all the wealth resources. It is one amongst those resources that feels limited in nature. We all know when we have it and that we are investing it with every passing second, we can also get lost in time when we are doing something pleasurable. We can't for sure say how much time we ultimately have before we die. So when we share this limited precious resource with someone, it should be a transaction worth having with full awareness and conscious decisioning. We cannot earn this wealth back, nor can we generate more of it hence it is the most precious of all.

#2 - Health Wealth

Health is wealth because to earn material wealth, we will need to be in healthy condition physically, mentally, emotionally, psychologically, and so on. All of these different dimensions of our being are included in our health and wellness wealth. When we are healthy, we are positioned to become wealthy and enjoy that wealth. Many times, people possess material wealth and yet cannot enjoy it due to lack of health wealth. Due to sickness and other limitations, they are not able to rejoice in their material possessions fully and completely.

#3 - Financial Wealth

Money is the common language everyone in the world speaks. We are all mentally wired to earn money as a source of living, because the value of money and its importance in our life has been passed on to us genealogically. Money is the tangible form of wealth that we can earn, multiply, and share. It gives us a sense of security because it empowers us to transact with others in return for a valuable product or service.

#4 - Relationship (Family / Friends) Wealth

This is perhaps one of the wealths that we take for granted. We all know that having friends and family is a blessing, we often do not fully realize their value until we lose them. Having someone around us who supports us and cheers for us is priceless. Wealthy are those who have such people in their lives, around them at all times.

#5 - Spiritual Wealth

Attending the needs of the soul is one of the most gratifying experiences in life. Wealthy are those who spend time in silence, do the inner work, and tend to their soul. Spiritual and mental wellbeing are cornerstones of a successful life and are often the foundation on which all other riches lie.

#6 - Business / Profession Wealth

The work that we do brings us more than just money. Recognition is a big motivator. Job satisfaction, rewards, empowerment, confidence, etc. are all instrumental in our overall success professionally. When we have something to do, we have nothing to worry about. Doing meaningful work and working towards a purpose greater than ourselves is a great form of wealth.

#7 - Creative Wealth

Creativity is a natural phenomenon. It is the power of the brain that requires continuous nudges and freedom of expression. When we become curious and want to learn more, we grow and expose ourselves to a world of possibilities. Expressing ourselves creatively is more important than we will ever know. Everyone is creative whether we believe it or not.

#8 - Experience Wealth

The luxuries we enjoy in life and the experiences we have are a special kind of wealth. Unfortunately, those who can afford luxurious experiences don't always balance their time wealth in order to have those experiences. Experience Wealth isn't just about money. The time we spend in nature is definitely a big part of Experience Wealth. There are many experiences we can enjoy without including money. Cuddling on the couch with our kids, having a picnic with our spouse, visiting local sites, enjoying a free concert in the park, etc.

Experience Wealth also includes buying a house and the experiences we have in that home. The food we eat can be experienced by eating slowly. Travel is another way to experience and enjoy life. These are just a few examples of how Experience Wealth makes us richer and able to live more abundant lives.

In closing, I encourage you to not equate wealth and prosperity with money alone. There are several key factors that help us determine the overall opulence that we enjoy in life. These riches in totality make us feel peaceful, abundant, happy, and joyful which is what we all ultimately seek.

Values

Our values are a fundamental belief or the 'filter' we

have in our minds, which help us measure our success and satisfaction in life. When the things we do, the words we say, and the thoughts we have... align with the beliefs we hold... we feel satisfied and are content that our values are being met. On the contrary, when what we say or do... does not align and match our belief system... we feel unhappy, displeased, and conclude that our values are not being met and therefore our life is not turning out the way we want.

Values are a crucial part of our overall personality that dictates how we act, what we do, and why we do it.

Values are a fundamental part of our mental make-up and exist whether we realize it or not. They in fact don't merely exist, they also define the way we feel and act. We hold values that outline our behavior at home, work, in society, and so on. All of them surround our personal values. Our core values are the ones that formulate our perspectives in life. Below you will find a value exercise with five prompts to help you identify what you value the most in your life. These values define the quality of your life and make you happy.

Value Exercise

Prompt #1 - List the Things That Make You Happy

Think deeply about what exactly makes you happy. Visualize the exact scenario of when you were the happiest and everything that was surrounding you when you were happy in terms of people, places, things, situations, and events.

Prompt #2 - List Every Memory That Fills You with Pride

What is the thing that makes you feel the proudest about yourself and/or about others in your family or with your friends? When was it that you felt you made it, you achieved it, or did something significant that changed or improved your life.

Prompt #3 - Write The Times You Felt The Most Fulfilled

When you felt the most satisfied. What gave you a sense of peace and achievement? List any specific events that occurred in life that made you feel that way. Was it something you did or that someone did for you that made you feel relaxed and situated?

Prompt #4 - Reminisce About Situations When You Felt Happy, Proud, and Fulfilled

Using your answers from Prompts #1 - #3 above:

Was there a commonality in them?

Did they all occur at the same time or at different times?

Write about the things you were doing, seeing, hearing, and feeling in those situations.

Prompt #5 - Now Imagine Your Life Without Those Situations

What are the things you listed for Prompts #1 - #3 above that you cannot imagine your life without? Think why each and every experience, emotion, and feeling is truly important and memorable for you. What needs to happen now in order to create more of those things? What do you need to do more of to have those pleasant experiences in your life? Would you do them even if they weren't popular or deemed important by others?

Once you have identified all those things above, you will be able to determine the common thread of values that define the way you feel, experience, and express yourself in your life.

Now that you have listed your values, the next step is to prioritize them. Look at everything on your list.

Go within and ask yourself: "Which one is the most important to me?"

Put #1 next to that value.

Continue by looking at your list and asking yourself the same question. Put #2 next to your answer.

Make your way through the entire list.

What are your top 5 values?

Everything I do is governed by my top 5 values: #1 Making a difference, #2 Positivity, #3 Empathy, #4 Inner Harmony, and #5 Happiness.

Understanding your values is a very important exercise that will help you make the right decisions in life. These are the decisions that will make you happy and feel satisfied.

Your core values are a central part of your existence and will always guide you to make the right choices. Let your values be your guiding light in life with full awareness and responsibility.

Empathy

As I mentioned above, my third value is Empathy. I will expand further on this subject here because it is an important life skill that we all seek. It can also be a bit of a challenge. Empathy is the practice of sharing other people's feelings and it's a two-way street. At best, empathy is reciprocal. It is a wonderful thing to give empathy and a very delightful thing to receive. In personal, professional, as well as social life… empathy or lack thereof… makes a huge difference.

A recent people survey concluded that eighty-five percent of those surveyed desired to be more empathetic. Highly empathetic people are sensitive, intuitive, and very charismatic. Nine out ten people find that they are better persons when they practice empathy, and it is not surprising at all that ten out ten people said they benefited from other people's empathy.

Empathy can be developed by getting in tune with ourselves and others around us. People tend to gravitate towards others who provide them the space to be themselves and express themselves fully. Look for emotions and vulnerability. These are the signs that a person needs a bit of empathy and a helping hand. They are the most receptive during times like these. Don't be afraid to show your own vulnerability, because it helps to build trust.

Typically, we only see the outer expression of people. Imagine yourself in their shoes. Empathy is about going a level deeper and trying to understand the 'why' behind the 'what' of other people's behaviors. Listen more than you speak. When we listen, we are allowing others to speak and express themselves. This allows them to feel lighter and better. Once they're done speaking, they are more receptive to our advice and/or opinions.

Avoid making assumptions. When we start assuming, we let assumptions take the place of factuality. In any relationship, trust is a must and assumptions kill that.

If it's so sought after, why isn't empathy the norm? There are a few challenges in practicing empathy...

It is time consuming. In today's world, waiting is wasting. We have no patience and unfortunately understanding someone's viewpoint doesn't fit well with our 'drive thru' mentality. Being empathetic requires us to give one hundred percent attention to the other person.

It also requires us to let go of our egos. When we are looking at things from another person's point of view, we get to let go of our point of view, which is not always very intuitive nor is it easy.

It requires us to be forgiving. Sometimes there is a history of hurt or misunderstanding with another person, be it at work or at home and it becomes difficult to let go of that memory and listen to them wholeheartedly.

Empathy is going to be even more important in the days to come, since remote work is going to be even more prominent post pandemic. In the near future it is going to be more critical than ever that teams operate in sync... despite the physical distance... and for that reason alone... trust building is going to be a must. Empathy will help build that bridge between remote teams and the organization since it is *impossible* to automate or outsource empathy.

Empathy During Pandemics & Other Challenges

"I don't want others to understand me" said no one ever. It's the human desire to be understood and loved by all. Empathy is a practice of understanding others, acknowledging their pain, and standing by them.

The same sentiment exists between an employer and an employee. They both want to be understood and need each other, especially during testing times such as the coronavirus pandemic. Below you will find EQ (Emotional Intelligence) tips for employers and employees.

EQ Tips for Employers

Conduct video town halls, all hands meetings, etc. and reassure one and all that we are #inthistogether. As a leader be vulnerable and share your personal experiences. This will encourage others to also express themselves which builds trust.

Acknowledge the hard work and dedication of the entire team - every single person. Until a pandemic is under control, we all fight an invisible enemy. We all have a version of our own pandemic struggle that is unique to us and our families.

Encourage one and all to take care of themselves and their families. Suggest time off as needed. Work can wait. Stress the importance of attending to kids and family.

Provide discounted or free subscriptions for online kids' classes, webinars on wellness, etc. Staying healthy is never canceled and should be a priority always, pandemic or not. Providing some free or discounted resources to employees and their kids during this time will be well appreciated and build loyalty.

Communicate timely updates, conduct check ins on the situation and how it will affect the company. There are multiple sources of information out there. The reliability factor is not the same for all of them. It is important to share trusted news and updates with teams and colleagues when possible. Also inquire about the anxiety and stress team members and colleagues might be facing during times of uncertainty, especially in-regards to their job security and personal safety.

EQ Tips for Employees

Share each other's work. Lend a helping hand whenever possible. Due to cancellations or pauses on multiple initiatives across the organization and the country, many colleagues have additional time during a pandemic to be helpful to others. Reach out to the teams where you believe you can add value. Cross out of the swim lanes and use those transversal skills to your advantage. There are many out there who need your help, especially the communication and social media teams.

Keep your team posted about your availability. Everyone's schedules are going to be impacted to some degree in this unique situation. While working remotely, it is important to be transparent and keep others posted of your availability to set realistic expectations.

Perform your tasks with integrity, knowing that the organization is counting on you and needs your contribution. Micro-management is a pain. The good news is that we can avoid it by building trust and being transparent. Employees can take responsibility and ownership of their tasks and demonstrate integrity. They will be awarded with autonomy and trust.

Be flexible about changing directions from the management. Remember that during a crisis everyone is attempting to be as nimble as possible and responding to happenings as quickly as they can. There are many things that are not in their control and things can change rapidly. Trust that your management team has your best interest in mind and will be focusing on time sensitive, critical tasks first.

Stay focused on the customer experience and proactively share thoughts and ideas to improve that experience. Absolutely nothing can or should take away the focus from the end consumer. Every person in the organization, regardless of customer facing or not, regardless of management or not, needs to keep the customer experience at the center of all decisions they make and all actions they take.

In a nutshell... when we lean on one another and practice kindness, the divide between work and personal life diminishes, the relationship between employer and employee improves, and we are able to be humans first and relate with each other at that level.

Womanhood Is a Matter of Pride

I believe it is a privilege to be a human. I also believe that it's an additional privilege with a cherry on the top, to be a human that can act as a medium to bring other humans to life.

I'm very grateful for a lot of things in life. The most important thing I'm grateful for is being and identifying as a woman!

I believe it is futile for women to fight for equality. It is like fighting to equalize apples and oranges. The only commonality between them is that they are both fruits. Similarly, the only commonality between a man and woman is they are both humans. However, they both differ in appearance, choices, behavior, and expression. Also, at the same time, I'm in no way discounting the similarities in mindset, achievements, and professional capabilities between both these sexes. This is actually more about masculine and feminine energy.

There is no doubt that women are expressive, vulnerable, and welcoming to others. In addition, women have three unique abilities that give them an edge over their male counterparts. These abilities make them a true leader without even knowing it. These are endurance, adaptability, and inclusivity.

Ability #1 - Endurance

Women are the strongest, most resilient human beings. Right from bearing a child to dealing with the problems that arise monthly and yearly to prep the body for childbearing is awe worthy. The strength to face the world, the strength to stand up for oneself for her family, and for her kids is in every woman's DNA. Women of all sizes, ages, and races are strong in their own right. They row their own boat, ride their own bike, drive their own car, and run their own families. Women lead teams, organizations, schools, businesses, and countries. They are making a change in the lives of themselves as well as others. Each time a woman stands up for herself, she inspires many other women to do so too.

Ability #2 - Adaptability

Women adapt to change unlike anyone else. No one other than a woman has the heart to accept their partner's family as her own. Back in the day, women used to move to their male counterpart's house and what a challenge that must have been. Living with a whole new set of people and a new lifestyle amidst new family culture. The strength of adaptability also shows up in a woman's life when she is juggling between work, life, social commitments, kids, and their schedules, etc. In a heterosexual parenting equation, there is an unsaid rule with a skewed responsibility share favoring the men. Women are clever and realize that it is better to change themselves than to change others.

Ability #3 - Inclusivity

Let's take a look at what this one means to a woman. She takes on the name of her husband and his family name without any inhibition and owns them. She makes them an important part of her life, her identity, and strives to become an important part of the family. Women know how to give, appreciate, celebrate, and cooperate with others more than anyone else. Women know the pain of not feeling included and have strived for generations to gain a 'seat at the table'. Women are empathetic and know that when we do not include everyone, we are less, we are weaker, and more vulnerable.

Women are...

Experts at what they do
Smart and successful
Model employees
Ready to fly

Women...

Have the right attitude
Row their own boat
Focus on what they can do best
Know the power of a team and have a team spirit

I encourage men to recognize, appreciate, and respect the women in their lives. Hats off to the women who have secured equal pay and job opportunities as their male counterparts.

Approaching the Job Seeking Process

Job seeking is often a long and daunting process with its own ups and downs. Every job seekers' journey is identical for the most part. Let me explain.

Their frustrations are alike
Their pain points are alike
To a great extent their outcomes are also alike

The best way to stand out is by having patience, perseverance, and maintaining a positive attitude.

Mantra: "I will find my dream job through patience, determination, and diligence."

As job seekers we often think of ourselves as the one 'on the seeking side', the 'wanting side'. We tend to forget that we have something valuable to 'give' in exchange: our time, our talent, and most importantly our personalities. We give what we have and therefore it is important to have the things worth giving. It's about time we change the conversation and recognize that an employer – employee relationship is more like a barter exchange and not a favor. You exchange skills, time, and energy for money.

When we are out there searching for a job and dealing with rejections and disappointments, we can still positively approach the job seeking process. Below you will find job seeking tips and how to overcome rejections.

Review Organizational Needs & Your Skills

Before applying for each and every job that appears on the job portal, within your domain or expertise, take time to review what it is that the organization is looking for. Meditate upon ways you can help meet those needs and provide resolutions. It is important for our skills to be complementing the needs of the organization and for us to feel fulfilled in our roles. After all that's what employers are looking for – 'the perfect match'. Someone that matches with the organizational requirements and not just from a skills standpoint, from a culture, value, and growth standpoint as well.

Empathize with the Interviewer

As a jobseeker your frustration is real. I'd like to encourage you to empathize with the interviewer's state of frustration as well. Just as you are tired of finding the 'right fit' for your career, employers are also tired of finding the 'right fit' for their organization. Communication is the key here. There needs to be clarity for both the employer as well as the job seeker. You both need to understand where the gaps are and why this work relationship will or will not work. With clear communication connections are made.

Always Focus on Providing Value

Focus on how you can add value to the organization during the job application process, the interview, and post interview thank you email. This is possible when we have an optimistic mindset, when we are confident, and when we are solutions oriented. It has been proven with a great success rate (more than eighty percent) that when the interviewee focuses on scalable, practical solutions they create a positive impression.

Know who you are and what motivates you. A YouMap Assessment with a certified YouMap Coach can help to identify your core strengths, values, preferred skills, and personality type. A thorough understanding of how all of these factors are intertwined together and how they show up in your life is critical. Also, the clarity on the impact that these four aspects have on your overall work life balance, brings in heightened self-awareness and focus that will empower you to streamline your job search, and identify the ideal job for you.

Reflect on the interviewing experience and focus on ways to improve the job seeking process in a way that can help you keep your spirits high, change your outlook, and help maintain a positive mindset which is the foremost requirement for any job seeker.

Opinions - What they are and why they matter!

Opinions are truly just that - opinions. They are not the final decisions and most definitely not the truth. Opinions are fleeting in nature and keep changing due to time, place, environment, and other contextual, socio-economical, and psychological factors. Therefore, they should be looked upon as varied viewpoints based on judgments and should not be taken to heart.

When we pay heed to opinions, more than they are worth, we face these issues…

Low Self Confidence

When others start sharing their opinions in-regards to your actions, words, and intentions, you will invariably start judging your own capabilities and start feeling less confident.

Indecisiveness

Once our confidence is shaken, we start questioning our every single move and action. We let self-doubt creep in and move us into analysis paralysis and inaction.

Lack of Initiative

Due to opinions that we receive, solicited or unsolicited, we tend to fear taking on new initiatives or exploring new ideas. We do not want those ideas to get rejected and our ego to get hurt. Therefore, we start piggybacking on someone else's ideas rather than initiating our own.

All the above traits have one common denominator. Repetitive opinions and commentary that instill FEAR. Fear restricts our actions, harms our creativity, and hurts our morale. If that fear is not addressed and resolved with urgency it creates a mental, physical, and psychological discomfort that eventually causes some severe long-term implications.

How to stay away from being a "football" of other people's opinions…

Self-Awareness

Knowing who we are and what our innate strengths and weaknesses are helps us be true to what we can do and how much effort we need to put in to be where we want to be. Other people's opinions do not bother us when we are aware of our true self.

Sense of Responsibility and Ownership

When one takes full responsibility for their own actions as well as inactions, they do not get bothered by other people's opinions. That is because they are fully conscious of the fact that they gave it their best shot and take full ownership of the outcome. They are aware there is a lot to learn. They derive satisfaction by giving one hundred percent each time in everything they do.

Empathy

Our ability to empathize is a huge strength that differentiates us from others and helps us understand and appreciate many different points of view. When we approach the situation from an empathetic angle, we realize all the different possibilities of a given scenario. Operating from empathy sheds a new light on a situation or event. Empathy also helps keep our ego in check by remembering and believing that all contributors have positive intent and that there could be more than one way to look at things.

Opinions, when provided in a constructive manner, help with 3 aspects...

Aspect #1 - Growth

Self-awareness is the foundation of growth. When we hear varying opinions on a certain topic, we learn about new possibilities that we didn't think existed or were achievable. That's personal growth. Many times combined opinions of key elements of the society help to bring about a change of reform as well. Like-minded people, whose opinions on certain issues match, can join forces to turn their vision into a reality. That's the growth of society at large.

Aspect #2 - Gain Perspective

We tend to learn a lot from the people around us. It is said that a collective mind is much smarter and more powerful than an individual mind. Rightfully so. In a collective setting, where people share the same vision and have similar opinions in-regards to execution or tactics, it opens up a dialogue and encourages creative thinking that makes the process enjoyable. This mental and cultural diversity helps widen our perspective and opens our mind to new avenues and possibilities.

Aspect #3 - Become a Team Player

It takes a lot of humility to hear opinions about our work or actions done with great intent in mind and to the best of our ability. Constructive opinions encourage us to think differently and to accept ideas and perspectives shared by others. Oftentimes opinions help us change part of our process and enhance it for the better. This enables us to work with each other's strengths in a group setting and join forces to bring ideas to fruition.

We all have opinions and make frequent judgments about other people, our society, and various issues. Let's remember that no one is entitled to our opinions just as we aren't entitled to theirs. No one 'needs' to fit into our criteria and we don't need to fit into theirs. Take opinions with a grain of salt, take feedback a bit more seriously, and take your self-awareness very seriously. We can only grow and become a bigger, better person by being fully aware of where we stand today. Let's take the journey inwards first in order to grow outwards.

Mantra: Go inward to grow outward.

Use your discretion and make this a life worth living – the way you deem appropriate, on your terms, no opinions attached – for we get only one life and it's too precious to be wasted on bothering about other people's opinions – for that's what they are at the end of the day – opinions and not facts!

Personal Branding Traits

Personal branding is the act of being consistently authentic in all areas of our lives. Social media is an extension of who we are. Famous people have built businesses that thrive on the reputation they have built for themselves. In other words, the way they show up every day. They are able to enjoy the riches and also leave behind a legacy.

Build a personal brand and leave a legacy. Below you will find ten remarkable traits that one needs in order to build a noteworthy personal brand.

Trait #1 - Being Focused

When we are clear on who we are and what we stand for it helps our audiences to understand what value we can potentially add to their lives. People are able to relate with us better if we are focused and have clarity of vision, action, and interaction.

Trait #2 - Being Vulnerable

Vulnerability is a blessing and requires courage. One needs to have reached a state of mental peace and confidence to be vulnerable, especially when one is a successful entrepreneur and is deemed a thought leader. Leaders are not shy to share their weaknesses or failures just because their reputation becomes questionable. They are aware and responsible enough to know that being real is more important than being right. They are fully cognizant about the fact that they are prone to error, and do not claim to be error free or godly.

Trait #3 - Being Effortless

It is easy to spot someone putting in a lot of effort and trying to be someone s/he is not. That's not the case with leaders that are confident and comfortable in their own skin. One should live his/her values to the fullest and never violate the values of others. Firmly believing that happiness and success are for everyone and are abundant in nature, which is the true secret here.

Trait #4 - Being Relatable

Relatability comes from being authentic, raw, and present. Lack of pretense is the key to connecting deeply with others. It is important to build that trust with people who can see a bit of themselves in us. We get to connect with our audiences at a human level where no boundaries exist when it comes to age, sex, origin, nationality, preferences, etc. Documenting our journey and sharing a 'slice of our life' with our audiences, helps them to connect with us, and want to join our communities and/or movements.

Trait #5 - Being A Storyteller

In our extremely chaotic business world today, audiences seldom have the time and patience to hear a monologue. They want to be involved and be part of the discussion or the narrative. To create a dialogue and have the interaction going both ways is really the intent here. Keep the communication channel open at all times and ever evolving. Create questions in your social media posts and make sure to comment on the responses you receive.

#6 - Being Tech Savvy

Technology plays a very critical role in our growth and reach in today's society. To ensure we are top of mind at all times and have our voices heard, we get to make ourselves available across all mediums of consumer touchpoints where our potential target audience lies.

#7 - Being A Community Builder

When we are not 'in it' just for gaining popularity and

propelling our business growth, it shows. Instead of focusing on fan following, one needs to direct his/her efforts towards helping others move forward and supporting them in their journey by 'sending the elevator back down'. The idea here is to bring like-minded folks together to foster support and collaboration without being self-centered.

#8 - Being Omnipresent

For building a strong personal brand, we get to connect with people across all channels and strata of society. We get to consistently show up for ourselves and others on all occasions.

#9 - Being Equivalent

Our online and offline presence should be an extension of who we are and should not differ in nature. We get to walk the talk and demonstrate our thought leadership and authenticity in public and business interactions. Our personal branding should not differ from who we are as a person. Rather it should be an extension of who we are intrinsically.

#10 - Being Composed

Along with becoming popular and desirable, building a personal brand also makes us prone to trolls and public scrutiny. It is very critical in a situation like this to keep our cool and respond to applause. When trolls strategically have nothing to respond to, they eventually go away. The internet never forgets, therefore it's critical to act responsibly at all times.

In a nutshell, personal branding is about documenting and sharing how we continuously evolve personally and professionally. It's a way of life and an interesting one at that.

Corporate Success – Done Right!

It's an amazing sight to see that the corporate world is growing up, strength by strength, with more and more leaders focusing on authenticity and mental health. Heightened awareness and availability of jobs in the marketplace, contribute tremendously towards this new growth. Work hours and location flexibility add up to make working in the corporate world more doable.

10 Personality Traits of Successful People in the Corporate World

I have identified 10 personality traits of successful people in the corporate world...

Trait #1 - They have a charming personality

Trait #2 - They tend to have a smile on their face at all times

Trait #3 - They are always looked upon as successful and approachable

Trait #4 - They have a collaborative mindset

Trait #5 - They always empower others

Trait #6 - They encourage others to share their ideas, point of views, and opinions without being judgmental

Trait #7 - They possess a team spirit with team unity being of utmost importance

Trait #8 - They live up to the old adage 'united we stand, divided we fall'

Trait #9 - They have a mindset that helps to build trust and motivation within a team

Trait #10 - They promote a sense of ownership and responsibility

How does a leader stand apart in a competitive market?

Successful People

Successful people have a *can do - challenge accepted -* attitude. Conflicts arise in every organization at every level, and in every industry.

What makes a true difference and helps us tackle any situation better is the, *can do - challenge accepted -* attitude.

A fearful approach to any situation leads to loss of confidence and the inability to think things through. People who consider a problem to be bigger than it truly is – end up giving up on issues that they could have indeed resolved. Successful people believe that they are bigger than the problem itself and not vice versa. Attitude is what makes all the difference.

Successful people possess confidence and courage. Many times, complex situations arise at work that require tough decisions to be made, and rather promptly. Decisions come with authority and authority comes with responsibility. The courageous take responsibility for their actions, choices, and decisions.

It takes courage to make bold decisions to hire or fire, go or no go, approve or disapprove, and so on. It takes confidence to believe that those decisions are aligned to the company's culture and policies. To rise up the corporate ladder, confidence and courage are a must.

Successful people have a calm and collected mind. Success can never come to a clouded mind. A calm and collected mind is of utmost importance in decision making, building interpersonal relationships, as well as building reputation and likeability with colleagues. A non-biased, non-judgmental person is sure to be looked upon as a well-respected leader.

Successful people get involved and make sure that their team understands that their success is the team's success. They are sensitive towards other people and make conscious efforts to not hurt anyone's feelings. Their actions demonstrate respect and sensitivity towards their colleagues. They also try to be as helpful as possible.

Successful people know how to and do demonstrate continuous improvement. The most important precursor to growth is constructive criticism. It is very rare to find someone who can truly mentor us in the right direction. When such an opportunity presents itself, it is the most sensible to value that person's feedback and act upon it. Most leaders and mentors like to see that their feedback is taken seriously and that improvements are made or are visibly in progress.

Successful people maintain correct up to date documentation. This documentation might feel like an unimportant administrative chore. It actually acts as a shield. There are several instances in the corporate world wherein accuracy of documentation has saved a lot of trouble and many a lawsuit. It ensures traceability and gives one a sense of ownership. With that being said, it is important to save the documentation along with appropriate approvals into a shared location that is accessible and safe at the same time. It is also important to lock documents and track changes when shared.

Successful people are creative. To me creativity is the key to a stress-free work environment especially when it comes to solving problems. Problems are boring by nature. Tackling them doesn't have to be boring. Get creative in your problem-solving efforts. It is always important to look at a problem from different perspectives than the routine and solve them with improved ways that align with corporate policies.

Successful people provide complete closure to misinformation/issues/differences. To be successful you need to make sure that no issues are left open, no misinformation is being transmitted, and no differences exist within the team.

A complete closure is required to put issues to rest, learn from them, and make the necessary improvements.

Resolution also indicates that we have learned from the previous mistake and that the same mistake will not be repeated. Adopting a 360-degree approach, taking feedback from all concerned, will help build trust and a shared commitment to improve.

In a nutshell, success is success only when it's shared, only when it makes you humble, only when it makes you and people around you smile, and only when it lets you sleep in peace. There are many people that have got it right. You can too!

Success & Visibility

Success of every company in the world depends on the performance of its people, no matter what industry, size and location the company is in. There is no substitute for human capability. Luckily every individual is gifted with unique capabilities. Our gifts, passions, strengths, and dreams are distinct. Time and circumstances seem to erode this uniqueness, and we tend to get lost in the crowd. We forget our identity and become *invisible*. This stage is where I come in.

I help business owners and executives design the life and career they want by tapping into their Inner Intelligence so they can interrupt old habits, access their creative mind, and lead a balanced life with Radical Self Awareness.

My V.I.S.I.B.I.L.I.T.Y Framework is designed to take you on a journey of self-discovery that involves four important stages.

Stage #1 - Paying Attention to our current state (A.S.K)

Stage #2 - Setting a clear Intention of where we want to be (M.A.P)

Stage #3 - Manifestation of our goals into reality (A.C.T)

Stage #4 - Expansion of our horizon (O.W.N)

My clients receive clear processes and instructive guardrails to enhance complete blossoming of their innate nature and skills leading towards a holistic transformation.

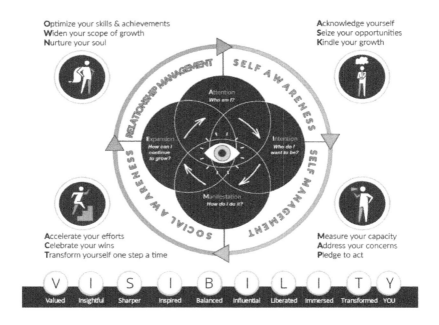

You can view this graphic on my website and join me for my Master Class: www.FalguniKatira.com

Stage #1 – A.S.K.

Stage #2 – M.A.P.

Stage #3 – A.C.T.

Stage #4 – O.W.N.

Stage #1 – A.S.K.

Acknowledge yourself

Seize your opportunities

Kindle your growth

Stage #2 – M.A.P.

Measure your capacity

Address your concerns

Pledge to act

Stage #3 – A.C.T.

Accelerate your efforts
Celebrate your wins
Transform yourself one step at a time

Stage #4 – O.W.N.

Own your skills and achievements

Widen your scope of growth

Nurture your soul

I have included journal prompts from the chart. Use the rest of the book to dig deeper.

Stage #1 – A.S.K.

A.S.K.

Acknowledge yourself...

Who are you at your core self?

What is your unique nature?

Why are you here?

Where do you want to go from here?

Who are you at your core self?

What is your unique nature?

Why are you here?

Where do you want to go from here?

A.S.K.

Seize your opportunities...

Who can help you get to where you want to be?

What skills will you need to help you grow?

Why do you want those growth opportunities?

Where are those growth opportunities?

Who can help you get to where you want to be?

What skills will you need to help you grow?

Why do you want those growth opportunities?

Where are those growth opportunities?

A.S.K.

Kindle your growth...

Who are the people that encourage you?

What are the characteristics of those people?

Why are they important to you?

Where do you find them?

Who are the people that encourage you?

What are the characteristics of those people?

Why are they important to you?

Where do you find them?

Stage #2 – M.A.P.

M.A.P.

Measure your capacity...

Who edifies you?

What do they say?

Why do you think they say that?

Where in your life can you do more of it?

Who edifies you?

What do they say?

Why do you think they say that?

Where in your life can you do more of it?

Where in your life can you do more of it?

M.A.P.

Address your concerns...

Who challenges you?

What do they say?

Why do you think they say that?

Where are your other triggers coming from?

Who challenges you?

What do they say?

Why do you think they say that?

Where are your other triggers coming from?

M.A.P.

Pledge to act...

Who can hold you accountable?

What are your goals?

Why are those goals important to you?

Where will you share your goals & with whom?

Who can hold you accountable?

What are your goals?

Why are those goals important to you?

Where will you share your goals & with whom?

Stage #3 – A.C.T.

A.C.T.

Accelerate your efforts ...

Who is in your way?

What can you learn from them?

Why are they a matter of concern?

Where can you avoid other pitfalls?

Who is in your way?

What can you learn from them?

Why are they a matter of concern?

What can you learn from them?

Why are they a matter of concern?

Where can you avoid other pitfalls?

A.C.T.

Celebrate your wins...

Who are your cheerleaders?

What do they say?

Why do they say it?

Where do you like to celebrate & with whom?

Who are your cheerleaders?

What do they say?

Why do they say it?

Where do you like to celebrate & with whom?

A.C.T.

Transform yourself one step at a time...

Who are your mentors & coaches?

What are your favorite learnings from them?

Why is transformation important to you?

Where will it take you from here?

Who are your mentors & coaches?

What are your favorite learnings from them?

Why is transformation important to you?

Where will it take you from here?

Stage #4 – O.W.N.

O.W.N.

Own your skills and achievements...

Who helped you to identify your skills?

What are the themes in your assessments?

Why are your achievements important?

Where can you expand your achievements?

Who helped you to identify your skills?

What are the themes in your assessments?

Why are your achievements important?

Where can you expand your achievements?

O.W.N.

Widen your scope of growth...

Who can take you to the next level?

What are some future growth possibilities?

Why are your goals expanding your growth?

Where can you expand your scope of growth?

Who can take you to the level?

What are some future growth possibilities?

Why are your goals expanding your growth?

Where can you expand your scope of growth?

O.W.N.

Nurture your soul...

Who is your spiritual guru?

What are your spiritual aspirations?

Why are they important to you?

Where do they fit in with your life goals?

Who is your spiritual guru?

What are your spiritual aspirations?

Why are they important to you?

Where do they fit in with your life goals?

ABOUT THE AUTHOR

As a Personal Growth Strategist and Certified Transformation Coach, Falguni Katira empowers leaders on their path towards holistic growth and success. Falguni's *Journey to Visibility podcast* brings inspiration from the VICTORY stories and personal experiences of various leaders. Her life's purpose is to create a ripple effect of radical self-awareness, bringing true joy and passion into the lives of others.

Falguni believes that all individuals are the torchbearers of culture and stewardship. Leaders who work with her are positioned to maintain their competitive edge in the face of global change.

Made in the USA
Middletown, DE
26 April 2021